WAY TO GREAT GOLF

GREG COMEAUX

& LARRY CANO

MASTERS PRESS

A Division of Howard W. Sams & Co.
A Bell Atlantic Company

Published by Masters Press (A Division of
Howard W. Sams & Company, A Bell
Atlantic Company)
2647 Waterfront Pkwy E. Dr, Suite 300,
Indianapolis, IN 46214

Printed in the United States of America.

96 97 98 99 00 01

10 9 8 7 6 5 4 3 2 1

**Library of Congress Cataloging-in-
Publication Data**

Comeaux, Greg.
    Stretch and strengthen your way to great
golf / Greg Comeaux & Larry Cano.
        p. cm.
     ISBN 1-57028-088-6 (paper)
     1. Golf--Training. 2. Stretching exercises.
I. Cano, Larry. II. Title.
GV979.E9C65   1996   96-12943
796.352'3--dc20   CIP

Contents

AUTHOR'S STATEMENT

The stretches, exercises and nutritional advice in this pocket guide are intended to be used in conjunction with lessons and advice on golf swing mechanics and game strategy available from your local golf professional, and should not be construed as a replacement for professional instruction. Any person with a medical or nutritional problem, or a pre-existing injury should consult a physician before attempting the exercises in this book.

Credits
Design: Steve Hale
Photography: Larry Cano
Cover Photography: Ron Warmbier

INTRODUCTION: A TOUGH SPORT REQUIRES GOOD HABITS

The sport of golf is growing in popularity by leaps and bounds, and more people are taking up the game like never before. Others, who might have once chased the little white ball, are returning to the course in record numbers. In fact, over 20 million people now play golf in the United States alone, and millions more play around the world. Many, however, refuse to accept the fact that the demanding game of golf is serious exercise. If the proper time and attention is not given to stretching, strengthening and nutrition, then one's scoring — and therefore one's sense of satisfaction and feeling of accomplishment — will never meet one's expectations.

Most amateur golfers run from their cars a few minutes before a round, check in, then dash to the first tee. A few twists and bobs and practice swings is all the preparation they do before picking up a driver, the toughest club in the bag, and attempting to play one of the most difficult games there is.

What separates golf from most other sports is that it takes four to five hours to play and it requires one to be both mentally and physically sharp the entire time.

In most other sports one utilizes bursts of energy with rest periods in between. Aerobic activity elevates the heart-rate and helps the body stay warm and loose. Endorphins kick in and propel one into a "zone" where the mind is calmed and instinct can take over.

But golf is different; there is no great aerobic effect derived, unless the course is wide open and one walks fast and is able to play quickly. The normal golf game is stop and go, stop and go. It can be a tedious exercise so golfers must use other tactics to keep loose and warm between shots in order to reach a "zone" where the mind is quiet and the body performs effortlessly.

If performance can be enhanced in fast-paced sports where there's literally no time to think, then the challenge in golf comes into clear focus. In golf, there is almost too much time to think and that can mean trouble. In golf, the opponent is oneself; we had better be both physically fit and mentally disciplined to play well.

We have all been on the way to a great round and have suffered a momentary loss of concentration or a physical breakdown that leads to a misfire. And WHAM!, the wheels come off, we take a double or a triple bogy, and that spectacular round starts to go right out the window. Correct stretching, strengthening and sound nutrition can go a long way to preventing costly physical and mental errors on the golf course.

By following our simple and easy methods you can improve your strength, agility, endurance, and mental focus.

A golfer attempts up to 120 shots, in addition to another 140 to 360 practice swings during an average round. Those swings require more stamina and concentration than we realize. How many amateur players break down from physical exhaustion on the back nine and literally limp into the clubhouse, leaving their good scores out there somewhere around the 15th or 16th hole?

Whether you're a weekend warrior, a competitive tournament player or a golf professional, you can improve your enjoyment of the game and your score by devoting a little time and attention to the information in this pocket guide. You don't have to be a "fitness buff" to make our method work for you. Playing one or two rounds a week, combined with good nutrition and the proper stretching and strengthening exercises in between rounds, will put you in tip-top golf shape and help you become the golfer you've always aspired to be.

Minimizing Injuries

Playing golf requires the body to twist and turn in unnatural directions using muscles not normally used in other activities. The golf swing transfers a tremendous amount of torque to the lower back, shoulders and neck, ankles and wrists. The repeated action can cause any one of these areas to break down. Unfortunately, unlike other sports whereby an athlete can "play through" an injury, an impaired golfer might as well hang up the clubs. It is nearly impossible to hit a golf ball consistently while in pain. An injury to a golfer will stay in the back of his or her mind and surely gnaw at his or her confidence and certainly affect performance. When your body is injured, your mind is also injured. A golfer needs to be 100% both mentally and physically, and that means being injury-free.

One way to avoid injury in golf is to properly warm-up and stretch before swinging the club, and then to maintain that stretch during the round. Stretching and strengthening on off days will help make your rounds more enjoyable and help you avoid serious injury.

STRETCHING

Start out by giving yourself an extra 15 minutes before each round. Use this valuable time to compose yourself, calm your mind and focus on playing good golf. Visualize yourself making good shots and get the feeling of playing well. Then do our stretching routine; it will do wonders for your mental attitude, your swing and your score.

Isn't it interesting when we step back to examine our golf habits? We willingly play a four or five hour game, yet refuse to take an extra few minutes beforehand to properly warm-up and stretch. Have you ever gone to a football game, baseball game or professional tennis match and failed to see the players warm-up beforehand? Certainly not. Then why do most amateur golfers think they can dash out and automatically be at the top of their game?

Begin your preparation on the way to the course while in your car. Often, the closer we get to the course, the more excited we become about the round we're about to play. Our heart rate goes up, our minds start to race and we begin thinking about all the terrific shots we're going to make and how low our score will be.

stretching

You'll improve your performance by making a conscious effort to control your nervous energy as you travel to the course. One great way to do that is to become aware of your breathing while preparing for your golf game. Take controlled breaths through your nose and stay calm! Center yourself by concentrating on your breath and imagine gathering your energy in your lower stomach area, at a point just below your navel. As in the martial arts, breath control can assist performance. (In fact, while performing our stretching and strengthening exercises and while hitting the golf ball, make sure you take moderate, non-forceful, but consistent breaths. Many times we tend to hold our breath while making a golf swing when controlled breathing will help dissipate nervous energy and help us stay loose.)

Once you arrive at the course, after checking-in and before hitting practice balls, we recommend that you perform our stretching routine. Again, it is vitally important that you allow plenty of time before your tee time to properly stretch before hitting your practice balls. Rushing through your preparation will only hurt you on the course.

Stretching is strengthening. The two go hand in hand. To achieve optimum physical performance, one must stretch diligently and regularly. Keeping the muscles, ligaments and tendons loose and pliable is critical not only in sports, but can help you stay healthy and increase longevity. The Chinese have known this secret and have practiced it for centuries. In China and Taiwan, in public parks and workplaces, one can see the daily practice of Tai Chi, Kung Fu and other exercises designed to improve flexibility and increase vigor. The Chinese generally practice their stretching and strengthening exercises early in the morning every day, and consider them an essential component of living.

Have you ever watched the top pros swing the club and noted the fluidity, rhythm and power of their swings? These players have spent many long hours working to become limber. Their flexibility allows for a minimum of wasted motion and creates powerful, consistent shots.

With the proper effort, so can you! Golf requires strength, flexibility, stamina and precise timing. These can only come from good body mechanics and good body mechanics are a product of warm, pliant muscles, tendons and ligaments.

When you allow a muscle to flex to its peak, then return to normal, you build strength and endurance along with flexibility. You lubricate the joints and get them ready for the two or three hundred swings they are about to make in an average round of golf. Importantly, proper warm-up helps put your mind at ease and tells your body that you're ready to go play your best. It is virtually impossible to "groove" a consistent powerful and accurate swing without persistently working on stretching and re-stretching the muscles, tendons and ligaments.

Since golf is a game one can play long into life, let's begin a routine that can last a lifetime. Whether you're young, a senior citizen or in between, let's get started now and build habits that will change your life for the better.

STRETCHING EXERCISES

Each exercise should be performed for a minimum of 30 seconds to a maximum of 2 minutes.

Special thanks to the Costa Mesa Country Club, Costa Mesa, CA.

Stretch #1

Hold your arms straight out gripping a driver, put one leg forward, half-bent, with the other leg straight back. At the same time bend over at the torso, giving yourself the full benefit of lower back and hamstring stretching.

stretching excercises

Do the same with the opposite leg, slowly stretching each side. This exercise is designed to stretch and loosen the entire back and hamstring areas giving you full flexibility, especially when driving the ball for longer distance. It's also good for rotator cuff stretch as well.

Stretch #2

Grip an iron with both hands at each end of the club, cross your feet and slowly bend forward until you feel the stretch in your calves, thighs and middle back regions.

stretching excercises

Then re-cross your feet and repeat. This stretch is especially good for long iron shots that require lower body flexibility and a good hip turn.

Stretch #3

With your feet spread shoulder-width apart, grip an iron and hold it behind your shoulders, and slowly move your left hand toward your right foot, hold the stretch, then rise back up slowly to the starting position. Now, slowly move your right hand toward your left foot and repeat the movement. This exercise is designed to stretch the inside leg muscles as well as the buttocks, hips, upper back and shoulder regions.

Stretch #4

Grip the head of an iron in your right hand, while holding the end of the club in the palm of your left hand. Push with your right hand while slowly turning your torso from right to left. Your left foot should be forward and your right foot should be extended back to allow for a full stretch of back and inner-shoulder

Stretch #4

regions, as well as the hamstring area. Then change the club from your right palm to your left palm and repeat, stretching the other side of your body in the same manner. This exercise will stretch and strengthen your rotator cuff to help avoid shoulder injuries resulting from over-swinging.

Stretch #5

With your feet spread shoulder-width apart, hold an iron behind your back at waist-level. Slowly turn one side of your body clockwise, holding the stretch, then turn back to the starting position. Then repeat in a

counter-clockwise direction. Stretch each side at least three to five times. This exercise will loosen both your biceps and upper-lat areas, giving you a lot more freedom of movement on your body turn.

stretching excercises

Stretch #6

With your feet spread shoulder-width apart and your right arm at your side, extend your left hand straight up and slowly bend to your right. Slightly push your right hip outward, then bend back to the starting position.

Repeat for the other side. This exercise keeps your hips, outer-triceps and shoulders loose and flexible. It's a great exercise for short iron shots.

stretching excercises

Stretch #7

With a partner standing in back of you, hold your arms straight out at your sides. Have your partner slowly pull your arms backward, being careful not to pull them too far or too

stretch and strengthen your way to great golf

fast. Feel the stretch in your center back and shoulders. Repeat two or three times. This is an excellent exercise in preparation for hitting the driver.

stretching excercises

stretch and strengthen your way to great golf

stretching excercises

With your feet shoulder-width apart, grip an iron at each end and hold it behind your back. Slowly bend forward at the torso, at the same time stretch your arms upward as high as possible. This exercise is good for the lower back, calves and hamstrings and is essential for anyone with a lower back problem.

Stretch #9

With your feet a little less than shoulder-width apart, bend at the knees while grabbing the tips of your shoes and slowly straighten your legs as much as possible. Go slowly so as

stretching excercises

not to injure your hamstrings. This exercise is used to loosen the lower back, hamstrings, calf and Achilles tendon areas, important for all aspects of the game.

Stretch #10

With your feet spread a little more than shoulder-width apart, place your left hand on your right shoulder and your right hand on

stretch and strengthen your way to great golf

stretching excercises

your lower left waist-line. Lift both hands on
and off your body while alternating one hand
high and the other hand low. Repeat back-
and-forth for a total of 15 to 25 repetitions
for maximum flexibility.

Stretch Series #11

stretching excercises

As this series of exercises illustrates, use opportunities on the course to achieve and maintain a thorough stretch between delayed shots.

stretching excercises

stretching excercises

stretching excercises

stretch and strengthen your way to great golf

stretching excercises

stretching excercises

stretching exercises

Stretch #12

Use these positions while lining up your putts on the green to keep yourself loose. They are very helpful for anyone with tightness in the middle and lower back regions.

stretch and strengthen your way to great golf

stretching excercises

Be sure to perform all of the foregoing exercises slowly to acquire a complete and thorough stretch for ultimate flexibility. Choose the exercises best suited for you according to your physical abilities or limitations. Do not over-do it and stretch beyond your capability. To learn proper stretching takes some time and effort; it does not happen overnight. Consistency is the key.

Utilize your downtime within a round to continue doing these stretches. That way you'll stay warm and loose and be able to maintain your flexibility as well as your confidence for 18 holes. When waiting at a tee box or on the fairway to hit your next shot, incorporate stretching into your pre-shot routine. You'll find it will do wonders for you.

As you wait on the green, or as you bend to line-up your putt, try to move your body and find those areas that may be tight and subtly stretch them. The crouch is a perfect body position to keep the back and spine stretched, especially if you can keep your heels flat on the ground.

Try to find those variances in body positioning that will maintain your stretch, but by no means try to force yourself into unnatural positions or attempt to put too much stress on an a specific area.

DO NOT EXTEND BEYOND THE LIMITATIONS OF YOUR AGE OR PHYSICAL ABILITY.

STRENGTHENING

PGA golfers now have a training trailer that follows the tour and helps keep the players fit and injury-free. It utilizes free weights and machines along with a training and medical staff. The rest of us golfers aren't as fortunate. We have to work on strengthening on our own.

With only a few hours of work a week between rounds or between practice time on the driving range, the following exercises will help improve your overall strength and stamina. Do them in concert with proper stretching, and you will develop increased energy and endurance to make your last approach shot as sound as your first drive. Not only will you feel and look better, but increased strength will make it easier to maintain consistently good swing mechanics, will add more power and distance to your game and will help you stay more focused mentally during your round.

We encourage you to walk the round whenever possible. When you walk, be sure to shift your bag frequently from one side to the other. That way you won't put undo strain on only one side of your body.

If for any reason you can't lift or carry your bag, use a pull cart. By walking over three miles over uneven terrain each round, you'll really begin to condition yourself and improve your lower body strength. Many golfers insist they play better when they walk — that they can get into the flow of the game easier and "see" the course better. Even when you must take a cart, such as when you play a popular course on a crowded weekend, for instance, trade-off riding and walking with your partner. That way you won't deprive yourself of the many benefits of walking.

STRENGTHENING EXERCISES

These exercises are designed to strengthen your muscles, not to build bulk. They will give you the strength and stamina needed for 18 holes of golf. Remember, strength combined with flexibility is vital no matter what the sport.

Use weighted dumbbells according to your physical capabilities. Not too heavy, not too light. Perform each exercise to a minimum of five repetitions and no more than ten repetitions for a total of three sets per exercise.

If you choose not to use dumbbells, isometrics is always a great alternative for strengthening. As with the stretching exercises, pick and choose from these exercises the ones that best fit your athletic ability, age and fitness level.

Seated Side Lateral Raises

With your arms at your side, slowly raise each arm up to shoulder level, then back down.

Seated Side Lateral Raises

This exercise is designed to strengthen the front, side and back shoulder regions to help avoid injury from the repetitive golf swing.

Lateral Raises with Partner

Perform this exercise with or without a partner. Without a partner, keep your back straight and the repetitions strict, with no swaying of the body at all.

Lateral Raises with Partner

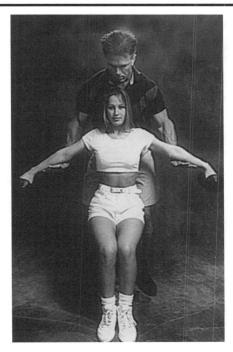

With a partner, hold his or her arms under the elbow and slowly help your partner raise their arms.

Isometric Lateral Raises

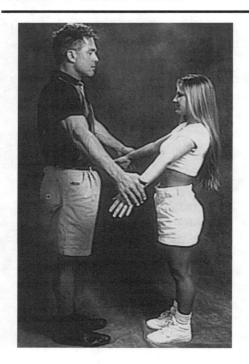

stretch and strengthen your way to great golf

Isometric Lateral Raises

Have your partner stand in front of you and have him or her apply downward pressure on the tops of your hands as you raise your arms upward and downward. To prevent shoulder injury, be sure not to apply too much pressure on the way up or on the way down. This is a great exercise for strengthening the forearms, biceps, and outer-shoulder areas.

strengthening excercises

Women's Push-ups

In doing push-ups for ladies, your knees should be on the ground with your feet off the ground. Keep your back straight as possible and place your hands shoulder-width apart.

Men's Push-ups

Place your hands shoulder-width apart and keep your toes on the ground. Your back should be straight while going down and coming up. Perform each repetition slowly with no bouncing motion. Push-ups are great for upper chest, shoulder, back and over-all arm strength.

Zottman Curls

Whether seated or standing, grip dumbbells in each hand with your palms facing inward. Slowly alternate lifting each arm up and down.

Zottman Curls

This exercise is excellent for biceps and forearm strength.

Standing or Seated Triceps Curls

Hold dumbbell in your hands above your head and lower the weight to the down position, then back up slowly.

Standing or Seated Triceps Curls

Seated Forearm Curls

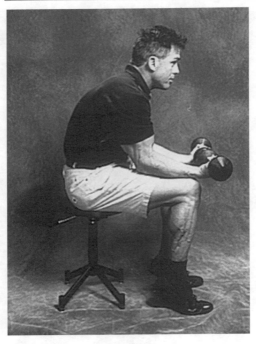

With your wrists facing upward, hold dumbbell in your hands on the edge of your knees. Slowly move your hands upward and

stretch and strengthen your way to great golf

Seated Forearm Curls

downward. This exercise is great for strengthening your wrists and forearms and will help you get the ball out of a thick rough when you need to.

Kick-Backs

With dumbbell in hand and torso slightly bent forward, move only your forearm backwards

stretch and strengthen your way to great golf

Kick-Backs

and foreward. Keep your body still and your upper-arm in place. This will keep your triceps strong and pliable.

Standing Biceps Curls

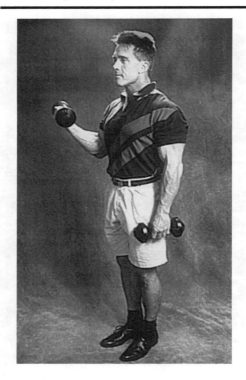

stretch and strengthen your way to great golf

Standing Biceps Curls

Grip dumbbells with your palms facing inward and hold at your sides. Alternately raise each arm while twisting your palms upward on the way up, and twisting your palms inward on the way down. This exercise is important for maintaining strong upper-forearms and biceps.

strengthening excercises

Straight-legged Deadlifts

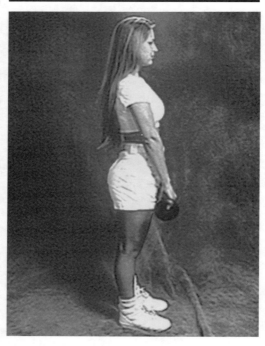

Stand straight, hold dumbbells in front of your thighs. Keep your back slightly arched and slowly bend foreward until dumbbells almost touch your feet or the tops of your ankles.

Straight-legged Deadlifts

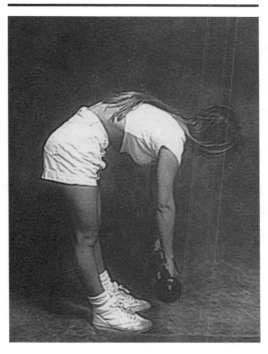

This exercise will strengthen your lower back, buttocks, and hamstring and calf areas. Lower body strength is an essential part of the golf swing. (BE SURE NOT TO USE TOO MUCH WEIGHT!)

Half Squats

With or without dumbbells, place your feet shoulder-width apart. Keep your back straight and slowly squat half-way down and come back up. Do not jerk or use fast movements

Half Squats

to protect your knees while strengthening your thighs and buttocks areas. (If needed for balance, hold onto a chair, see next 2 pages.)

Half Squats

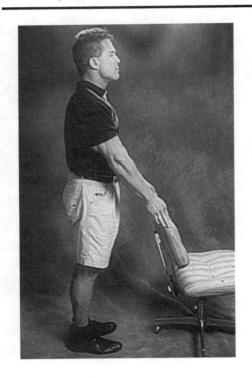

stretch and strengthen your way to great golf

Half Squats

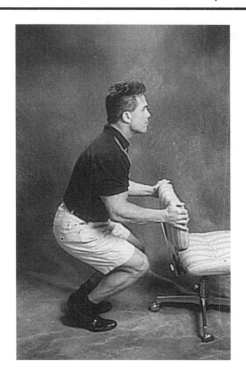

Calf Raises

Standing flat-footed, hold the dumbbells in each hand and slowly raise-up on your toes and then go back down. This exercise will

stretch and strengthen your way to great golf

Calf Raises

strengthen your Achilles tendons as well as your calves and help the walking golfer.

As with stretching, consistency is the key to making these exercises beneficial to you. Without use, muscles atrophy, so a little work every day is better than doing nothing at all. Be careful not to over-do it so you won't bulk-up and create tight muscles that will interfere with your golf swing. Our main objective is to help you strengthen and at the same time maintain that flexibility needed to play your best golf.

strengthening exercises

ADVANCED STRETCHING EXERCISES

The following stretches are ones that you can work on at home before and after your round or before and after performing the strengthening exercises. If you are new to stretching regularly, it is best to work on the previous stretching exercises for at least 30 days before attempting some of these advanced exercises. The advanced stretches are designed for you to do at home or at a gym. Use a stretching mat if possible, and try to work them into your daily routine. Listen to your body to locate any tightness, and concentrate on loosening those specific areas. Pay attention to your breathing and "breathe" into your stretch. As with the other stretches, don't stretch beyond your comfort zone. Remember, the more consistent you are in your stretching, the better results you will achieve.

EACH EXERCISE SHOULD BE PERFORMED FOR A MINIMUM OF 30 SECONDS TO A MAXIMUM OF 5 MINUTES.

Advanced Stretch #1

While standing with your weight balanced on your right leg, bring your left knee up as high as you are comfortably able to, and swing both arms across your body to your left side.

stretch and strengthen your way to great golf

Advanced Stretch #1

Now change legs and repeat to the other side. Be sure to take deep, even breaths through your nose. This exercise is excellent for keeping your hips loose and flexible for proper swing rotation.

Advanced Stretch #2

Advanced Stretch #2

While standing, cross your right leg over your left and bend down slowly and touch your fingertips to your toes. Keep your legs straight at the knee, being careful not to go too fast or to stretch beyond the limits of your ability. If you are unable to touch your toes, go as far as you can without putting any strain on the back of your hamstrings. Repeat, crossing your left leg over your right.

Advanced Stretch #3

stretch and strengthen your way to great golf

Advanced Stretch #3

Standing with your hands on your hips, lunge forward and outward at about a 45 degree angle with your left leg slightly bent. Now lock your right leg at the knee and slowly shift your weight out over your left knee. You should feel the stretch in your left thigh, your right hamstring and your lower back. Be careful not to shift too much weight forward at once or to move too quickly. Stop immediately if you feel any stress in your left knee. Repeat for the other side.

advanced stretching

Advanced Stretch #4

With your legs folded underneath you, place both hands behind you. Gently lean your head backward as you straighten your back and breathe deeply.

Advanced Stretch #5

Sitting with your legs folded underneath you, point your knees outward creating a "V." Clasp your hands together creating another "V" with your arms. Now rotate your upper body first to the left and then to the right as you would in your golf swing.

advanced stretching

Sitting comfortably with your back straight, grab your feet with both hands and pull them into you as much as you are able. Now move both knees toward the floor a few times to stretch your legs. Next, bend over slowly

Advanced Stretch #6

moving your head toward your feet. Bend downward as far as you are able to without putting too much stress on your back or on the inside of your thighs. Repeat.

Advanced Stretch #7

Spread your legs as wide as possible to stretch the inside of your thighs. Bend your torso slowly forward and try to place your elbows on the floor. Be careful not to stretch any farther than you're able. A little progress at a time will go a long way!

Advanced Stretch #8

Stretch your legs as wide as possible. Lean to your right side and grab your right leg with your right hand as far down on your leg as possible. Bring your left arm over from a higher position and also stretch it as far down your right leg as possible. Breathe slowly and deeply throughout the exercise. Repeat, stretching to your left side.

advanced stretching

Extend both legs straight out in front of you. Bend down slowly and attempt to touch your hands to your toes and hold the position for as long as possible. Be sure to breathe into the stretch!

Advanced Stretch #10

Extend your left leg out in front of you and fold your right leg in, assuming a "hurdler's" position. Move your right arm as far down your left leg as you are able to and attempt to touch your forehead to your knee. Again, don't worry if you are not yet able to stretch all the way down at first. With diligent practice, you will get there! Repeat for the other side.

Advanced Stretch #11

Extend your left leg out in front of you and with the help of your right arm, fold your right leg inward as shown. Grab your left knee with your left hand and slowly bring your head as far as you can comfortably toward your left knee. Keep breathing properly! Repeat for the other side.

Advanced Stretch #12

Lie on your back with your arms extended above your head. Pull your knees up to one side. Keep them there for a count of 5, then rotate them to the other side and again hold for a 5 count. Repeat.

Advanced Stretch #13

Lift your right leg up and grab it with your arms. Keep it as straight as possible. Now pull it into you gently and slowly, while maintaining your breathing. Repeat, stretching the other leg.

Advanced Stretch #14

Place your right leg on the seat of a chair, extending your left leg straight along side of it on the floor. Concentrate on your breathing. This is a great exercise for loosening your hip flexors and lower back. Repeat for the other leg.

Advanced Stretch #15

Extend your left leg straight out in front of you. Bend your right leg and place it over your left leg at the knee. Rotate your torso to the right and hold, placing your left hand to the right side of your body. Keep your spine straight and your head up. Hold for a count of 10. Repeat for the other side.

Advanced Stretch #16

Lie on your back with your arms at your side. Slowly raise your legs up and back until they are parallel to the floor. Hold as long as you can, then lower them back down to the starting position. Be sure to breathe slowly and deeply. You can vary this exercise by holding your legs in a shoulder stand position. As you progress, you may want to lower your toes completely to the floor when you are able. DO NOT ATTEMPT THIS EXERCISE IF YOU HAVE A LOWER BACK PROBLEM.

advanced stretching

Prop yourself up on your hands with your fingers pointing toward your feet. Point your toes and gently rise into the stretch, bending your head back with your nose pointing toward the ceiling. Watch your breathing, and as with the previous stretching exercise, DO NOT ATTEMPT THIS STRETCH IF YOU HAVE A LOWER BACK PROBLEM.

ADVANCED STRENGTHENING EXERCISES

After you have become familiar with the first series of strengthening exercises, you can then incorporate some of the following series of advanced exercises into your routine. They are designed to help you build abdominal and lower body strength, both of which are essential in golf.

Leg Extension

Start in the down position and squeeze your legs on the way up, not totally locking them out, and back down again. Being slow and

Leg Extension

consistent in your movement is essential. Perform 3 to 5 sets of 8 to 12 repetitions.

Squats

Stand with your legs spread approximately shoulder-width apart. Go down until your buttocks are almost parallel to the ground, then back up. Keep your head up and your back as straight as you possibly can. Squats

Squats

are unquestionably the best exercise for building lower back and leg strength. Perform 3 to 4 sets of 7 to 10 repetitions with or without weights. Use the amount of weight that will allow you to perform the movement without any strain to avoid an injury.

Lunges

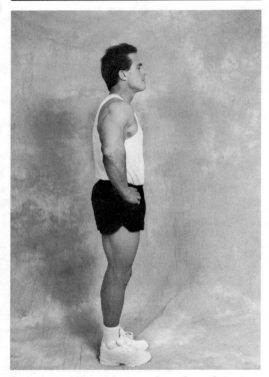

Stand straight with your feet 6 to 8 inches apart. Place one leg forward, slowly bending at the knee until that leg is parallel to the ground. Then return to your original position.

Lunges

Repeat with the other leg. Perform 2 to 4 sets of 7 to 10 repetitions for each leg. Doing lunges will help you with your balance, essential for a good golf swing.

Lunges with dumbbells

Holding dumbbells at your side, perform these in the same manner as described in the

Lunges with dumbbells

previous series. Perform 2 to 4 sets of 7 to 10 repetitions for each leg.

Good Mornings

Place a bar, with or without weights, behind your upper shoulders. With your legs a little less than shoulder-width apart, go down slowly until your torso is almost parallel to the floor.

Good Mornings

Then go back up again. DO NOT PERFORM THIS EXERCISE IF YOU HAVE A LOWER BACK INJURY. Perform 2 to 3 sets of 7 to 10 repetitions. Never use heavy weights.

Abdominal Crunches

With your head, back and buttocks flat on the floor, bend your knees so your feet are also flat on the floor. Put your hands behind your head and slowly crunch your head and stomach forward and upward, then back down again. You will feel your abdominal muscles

Abdominal Crunches

tighten. Doing this exercise regularly will go a long way towards preventing any back or lower back injuries. Strong abdominals promote a strong back! A strong back makes for a great golf swing. Perform 3 to 5 sets of 10 to 25 repetitions.

Crossover Leg Crunches

Same movement as crunches, except cross one leg over the other and touch the knee of the crossed leg with the opposite elbow. Cross

Crossover Leg Crunches

the other leg and repeat. This exercise is great for building upper back and upper abdominal strength. Perform 2 to 3 sets of 10 to 25 repetitions.

Lying Leg Raises

Lying Leg Raises

Lying flat on the ground, place your hands under your buttocks and slowly bring your knees up to your chest while moving your head forward. Move your head back down, while at the same time straightening your legs out. Keep your heels off the floor in the extended position if you can. Perform 3 to 5 sets of 10 to 20 repetitions.

PROPER NUTRITION

We realize that golf is a social game and that there's nothing more enjoyable than a hot-dog and a beer with the boys or girls at the 19th hole. But if you're really serious about feeling better and playing better golf, we ask you to apply some moderation to your golf course eating habits.

In the morning before play, limit caffeine and begin drinking three or four full glasses of water. Load-up on complex carbohydrates: oatmeal, granola, cream of wheat, pancakes, or scrambled egg whites with whole wheat toast. Try to avoid a greasy and fat-filled traditional breakfast with fried eggs and meat. Do what distance runners, football players or other athletes do before a big contest — LOAD UP ON COMPLEX CARBOHYDRATES! (In fact, eat plenty of complex carbohydrates the day before you play, if you can!) Remember, golf is a strenuous exercise, not just a walk in the park! Make sure there's enough gas in the tank if you're really serious about lowering your score.

While on the course, avoid those goodies available at the snack bar that are filled with sugar and empty calories. They will do absolutely nothing as a performance enhancer. They will get you up quickly, but will let you down just as quickly, causing you to become lethargic. Most snack bars at golf courses now offer an array of healthful alternatives from which to choose. Trail mix, bagels, pretzels, rice cakes, boiled eggs, granola bars, fruit and fruit juice all offer good, quick high-quality energy. If your course does not yet have these kinds of snacks available, suggest that they stock them.

Not only will the energy derived from complex carbohydrates affect you immediately, it will stay with you longer. You'll feel better physically throughout your round, and you'll be able to think clearly to avoid costly mental errors.

If your course allows you to carry-on your own food, we suggest that you pre-cook pasta, noodles, rice or baked potatoes to eat during your round. Make sure to use a container and ice that will keep them below 40 degrees to avoid spoilage. Snack on them at intervals when time allows BEFORE you become hungry. That way you'll assure that you'll have a constant store of energy when you need it.

You wouldn't go for a long hike without water, would you? Then why play golf without drinking plenty of water? Carry your own bottle and drink as much as you can throughout your round. Try not to drink alcohol while playing, but if you must, take in even more water, especially in the hot summer months.

We challenge you to put these nutritional ideas to the test. Follow our suggestions the next time you play. Eat oatmeal in the morning, pasta for lunch, fruit for snacks and see if you're energetic at the end of the round. See if you feel like playing a few more holes. We know you'll be pleasantly surprised.

A GAME FOR LIFE

If you want to play your ultimate golf game and become the player you've always wanted to be, we strongly recommend that you incorporate the simple methods in our pocket guide into your golf habits. Along with golf lessons and dedicated practice, proper stretching, strengthening and nutrition will help you mold that fluidity and consistency required to help lower your scores.

Remember, it is often said that we play the game of golf like we live life. That we exhibit our character and personality on the golf course. If that is true, isn't it about time we started changing the way we approach the game of golf — and improving our health and well-being at the same time? Use the stretching and strengthening exercises best suited to make your routine work well. Be consistent in your conditioning and we promise, not only will you start to play better golf, but you will also begin to play yourself into top physical condition as well. You'll look better, feel better and live longer.

Good luck and many happy rounds.

ABOUT THE AUTHORS

Greg Comeaux has played many different kinds of sports from wrestling to tennis, decathlon competition to backyard badminton. Whatever the sport, Greg has played it. Dedicated to personal fitness for the last 20 years, Greg has worked with virtually every type of athlete in almost every sport. Through it all, golf remained a constant passion. Growing up near Webb Golf Course in Baton Rouge, Louisiana, Greg started playing golf at eleven and has played continuously for over 29 years. As a six handicapper, he understands the mental and physical acuity needed to play the game well. The information contained in this pocket guide represents the culmination of years of Greg Comeaux's physical fitness expertise and golf experience and will change the way you play the game of golf forever.

Filmmaker and writer, Larry Cano has been playing golf for over 18 years and has studied the martial arts since 1973. Also an avid tennis player, Larry seeks to impart his understanding of elements of the internal martial arts — stretching, correct breathing, calming of the mind and energy control — to golfers to help them improve their game.

To contact the authors for seminars,
speaking engagements, or clinics,
or for information about
the upcoming video version of
Stretch and Strengthen
Your Way to Great Golf,
please write to:

Greg Comeaux & Larry Cano
P. O. Box 10095
Newport Beach, California 92658

NOTES

After you discover which exercises work best for you, this page can be used to design your own workout. Keep it handy when you go golfing.

Exercise	Page